Off-Campus Orientalism

Western University Branch Campuses in the Gulf

M.H. Ilias

GULF STUDIES PROGRAMME
India Arab Cultural Centre
Jamia Millia Islamia

AAKAR

OFF-CAMPUS ORIENTALISM
M.H. Ilias

First Published 2015

ISBN 978-93-5002-341-9

Published by
AAKAR BOOKS
28 E Pocket IV, Mayur Vihar Phase I, Delhi 110 091
Phone : 011 2279 5505 Telefax : 011 2279 5641
aakarbooks@gmail.com; www.aakarbooks.com

In association with
India Arab Cultural Centre
Jamia Millia Islamia
New Delhi 110 025

Printed at
Saurabh Printers Pvt. Ltd., A 16, Sector IV, Noida

Contents

1

Introduction

With the proliferation of international branch campuses,[1] GCC states are emerged as the new 'hub' of higher education in West Asia. The Gulf States' rise from the 'periphery' to 'centre' in the field of higher education is dramatic. Of the international branch campuses, establishing Western university off-campuses is the much-sought after trend with massive emulation throughout the region (except in Oman and Saudi Arabia), though the pace and magnitude vary from one country to another. Investment in this sector also has seen a dramatic increase in recent decades with the Gulf governments engaged in highly ambitious projects to put themselves on the 'global' education map. While primary and secondary education in the Gulf tends to follow national lines, higher education is very diverse with stakeholders from different parts of the world. American, Canadian, Australian, French and British universities have been established all over the region. In addition, Western-style methodologies and teaching practices are being employed in many of the state-run universities. With sophisticated and costly programmes

1. International branch campus is defined by Wilkins as an educational facility that has its own premises, where students receive face-to-face instruction in a country different to that of its parent institution. Stephen Wilkins, "Who Benefits from Foreign Universities in the Arab Gulf States?", *Australian Universities' Review* 53 (2011): 73-83.

of 'global standard', the Western universities are, in principle, established as a regional meeting point between the students from West Asia and global education providers.

The Gulf States have been the early takers of internationalization of higher education and the largest recipients of transnational institutions of higher learning whilst the British, American, Canadian and Australian universities have been the largest beneficiaries. A recent statistics shows that two-thirds (around 70) of the new universities founded in the Arab Gulf since 1993 are private, and most (at least 50) of them are branches of Western, mostly American and Western European, universities.[2] In UAE, where there is highest number of Western university off-campus (almost 40), the popularity of it is high.[3] According to the Higher Education Landscape Report 2012, student enrollment in Western universities inside the free zone in Dubai has risen by 11 per cent.[4] Another study indicates that Western university branch campuses in free zone have 46 per cent of the total number of university students in Dubai.[5]

Gulf governments find foreign universities attractive because they potentially generate non-oil revenue and provide educational opportunities for citizens and expatriates. Since the governments keenly seek to diversify both their academics and economies through bringing in Western university branch campuses, these institutions enjoy

2. Vincent Romani, "The Politics of Higher Education in the Middle East: Problems and Prospects", *Middle East Institute Viewpoints: Higher Education and the Middle East* 36 (May 2009): 2-3.
3. UAE hosts forty off-campuses of international universities. This is the highest number so far and it represents almost a quarter of all international branch campuses worldwide.
4. The Higher Education Landscape Report, published on 26 February, 2013.
5. Report published by the Knowledge and Human Development Authority (KHDA), *Gulf News*, 27 February 2013.

special economic and legal status and unprecedented funding. The primacy given to the private and foreign higher education ventures is evident from Qatar's pattern of spending in this field. In 2006, Qatar set out to raise its gross expenditure on research and development from 0.33 to 2.8 per cent of gross domestic product over a period of five years.[6] And the governments of Qatar and the United Arab Emirates have set up exclusive agencies for funding and providing facilities for these ventures.

The overwhelming support from the governments is actually to overcome the bitter experiences of other Arab countries that opened their academic systems to foreign and private so early in the 1980s as a part of improving the quality of education. The results have been problematic without proper backing of the state. Recent projects in the GCC countries have addressed this set of problems with the diversion of large chunk of state funding and government back up.[7] Over the last five years, the GCC countries have expended at least $50 billion on higher education.[8] In Qatar and UAE more than 50 per cent of the total expenditure in higher education is diverted to support foreign university projects.[9] Even Saudi Arabia which is otherwise the most state-centred country running eight public universities, joint the bandwagon with founding two private universities and numerous new private colleges. Although Saudi in the early days was very slow to accept this model, there are now clear signs of large investments.[10] However, Saudi does not rely

---

6. Salem Al-Khaldi, "Education Policies in the Gulf States", *Research Papers Series* (Dubai: Gulf Research Centre, 2007), 12-15.
7. Romani, "The Politics of Higher Education in the Middle East", 2.
8. Al-Khaldi, "Education Policies in the Gulf States",12-15.
9. Ibid.
10. Francois Therin, "Gulf: When will its Higher Education models Implode?", *University World News* 180 (2011): 17.

on foreign education institutions and is less in need of European academics.[11] Oman is also an exception spending considerably low amount in support of such ventures. The development in the field of higher education in Oman is represented only by the influx of new private colleges and universities run by the local groups. The levels of spending continue in UAE and Qatar reflecting a major trend; the emergence of the Arab Gulf as a heavyweight academic actor in the region.[12] But strangely enough, these two Gulf States do not have the requisite potential number of local students to cater the newly established Western universities.[13]

With the opening up of education system in the Gulf, there were actually two processes which were combined to each other; privatization and globalization.[14] While opened up the field of education for international players, local private initiatives were encouraged to counterbalance the growing concern about academic imperialism. This new "global regionalism" according to Olcott, plays an increasingly important part in the development of foreign partnerships and branch campus models.[15] However, the balance scenario did not yield a desired result as both the local private universities mainly with foreign partnerships and foreign universities ended up in an over-dependence on Western institutions, educational consultants and professionals.

---

11. Ibid.
12. Romani, "The Politics of Higher Education in the Middle East", 2.
13. Therin, "Gulf: When will its Higher Education models Implode?", 17.
14. Romani, "The Politics of Higher Education in the Middle East", 2-3.
15. Don Olcot, "Emerging Opportunities and Challenges for Regional Higher Education", *Middle East Institute Viewpoints: Higher Education and the Middle East* 36 (May 2009): 7-9.

The picture is not very rosy and the development of regional hubs for higher education is not without its challenges. While many take this development something that exerts a domino effect by improving the quality of education, others worry that it reflects yet another cycle of Western imperialism.[16] The recent influx of American and other foreign universities are, of course, sociologically and politically significant as they bring in not only an alien system of learning and pedagogy mismatching with the cultural and political milieus of the host countries but also a hegemonic oriental 'point of view' or 'gaze' in objectives and the way they function. The spread of Western university branch campuses is seen many scholars as a project of neo-colonialism seeking ideological and economic domination.[17] The globalization of education has also given greater mobility for elite Western universities and led to further inequalities, whereby the leading universities from Western Europe and North America establish a state of domination while the local universities in West Asia become increasingly marginalized. Orientalism in the context of branch campuses of Western universities in the Gulf also involves the extension of particular form of knowledge production that originated in Western Europe and are exported or imposed upon other parts of the world. Donn and al Manthri argue that the Gulf States become the consumers of a sort of orientalist knowledge and worldview rather than producers of a knowledge that lies at the root of their culture.[18]

There are several studies point to the severity of the

16. Ibid.
17. P.G. Altbach, "Globalization and the University: Myths and Realities in an Unequal World", *Tertiary Education and Management* 10 (2004): 1.
18. Gari Donn and Yahya Al-Manthri, *Globalization and Higher Education in the Arab Gulf States* (Dicot: Symposium Books, 2010), 12-17.

problems being faced by the higher education in the Gulf in the context of rise of Western university branch campuses. However, this paper's concern revolves around the fragmented practices through which new generation Western universities subtly endorse orientalism. Recurring ideas in this paper are evolved out of a series of field observations undertaken between 2008 and 2010 in Qatar and the UAE. Personal interactions with the students and teachers of Western universities in these two countries have also aided in developing the arguments presented here. Emphasis has been given to the opinions of Indian students studying in the Western university branch campuses in Qatar and the UAE. The field study, instead of being conducted along a structured interview/questionnaire model, employs a qualitative interactive mode. Regular informal visits and up-close personal interactions with them have helped in formulating the ideas about the exclusions of different sort. Methodology employed here, therefore, gives more importance to observations emerged out of personal interactions.

2

Origin and Spread

The entry of Western universities into other parts of the Arab world traces back to 1980s. Arab Gulf countries are actually the late takers of this trend which had a slow and hesitant beginning in the early 1990s with the openings of the American University in Dubai in 1990 and the University of Wollongong branch campus in Dubai in 1993.Soon after, Oman allowed the establishment of private higher education institutions, and Sharjah founded two universities in 1997.[19] Qatar also followed the suit by developing an ambitious project-Education City with branch campuses of the UK, the US and Canadian universities. In 2002, the Gulf University of Science and Technology became the first private university to open in Kuwait and following it Abu Dhabi struck deals with Paris-Sorbonne and New York universities to open branches. This shift was an offshoot of two parallel developments. When oil rich countries of the region began to diversify their economy by investing in the field of education, Western universities made it a point to globalize themselves further targeting the wealthy Gulf region as a prime destination for global expansion.

The course took a fast turn with the publication of *Arab*

---

19. John Willoughby, as quoted in James Calderwood "Western Universities Opening in GCC at Risk of Failing", *The National* 10 (April 2012).

Human Development Report by the United Nations Development Programme in 2003.[20] The report had some critical reference to the poor state of higher education throughout the Arab world. Part of the blame was gone to academic institutions in the region, with few exceptions, for their failure to produce enough qualified graduates with skills that served the needs of the emerging economy. The higher education sector across the region has routinely been criticized mainly for its inability to meet the needs of the industry. With mismatching educational profiles of locals, labour nationalization plans in many sectors like banking and hydro carbon remained a distant dream.[21] In order to overcome the situation, the report urged Arab states to invest massively in a sector that, it argued, "embodied the future of their societies.[22]" The report also highlighted the need of a knowledge society for the furtherance of economic growth. The pool of human capital for creating such a knowledge society, the report suggested, can be developed through a quality education system.[23] Although the publication of it ignited a revolution, the report prepared by Arab scholars came under severe criticism from other Arab intellectuals right from the beginning for its content and use of what were described as Western ethnocentric norms.[24] Anyway, what followed was a surge in higher education in the Arab Gulf region, along with its privatization and its

20. United Nations Development Programme (UNDP), *Arab Human Development Report 2003: Building a Knowledge Society*, (New York: United Nations Development Program Regional Bureau for Arab States, 2003).
21. Christopher Davidson, *Higher Education in the Gulf: Building Economies, Politics and Culture* (London: Saqi Books, 2008).
22. Ibid.
23. Ibid.
24. Olcot, "Emerging Opportunities and Challenges for Regional Higher Education", 7-9.

internationalization on an accelerated pace. This period also witnessed to a sudden increase in sending students abroad through scholarship.[25]

A long array of Western university branch campuses and private universities were soon established throughout the region. Eight universities were operating in Saudi Arabia in 2003, but at least 100 additional universities and private colleges have been created there since, and the country's annual budget for higher education has reached $15 billion, for 23 million inhabitants.[26] Kuwait and Bahrain also have a handful of transnational higher education providers. The GCC has now become home to branch campuses of several leading international universities, while-state owned universities have made collaborations of different sort with their counterparts in Europe and North America. A rough estimate says that today there are almost 100 branch campuses in the Gulf region alone with more concentration in the United Arab Emirates (Forty, of which twenty five are based in Dubai alone) and Qatar. Looking ahead to dwindling oil reserves, these two countries have set their sights on becoming 'knowledge-based economies' by 2030.[27]

The offshoots of established universities, mostly from the United States and Europe, were primarily invited by the region's governments to supplement their higher-education system, which they realized old-fashioned and could not

---

25. Davidson, *Higher Education in the Gulf*
26. Zvika Krieger, 2007, "Dubai, Aiming to Be an Academic Hub", *The Chronicle of Higher Education* 54 (October 2007): 8.
27. In 2006, Qatar set out to raise its gross expenditure on research and development from 0.33% to 2.8% of gross domestic product over a period of five years, although no data are available to verify whether it has achieved this goal. See Romani, "The Politics of Higher Education in the Middle East", 4.

attract the best-qualified students.[28] The focus has previously been given on undergraduate courses in mainly applied or professional subjects—engineering, medicine and business studies, for example.[29] With emphasis on research, the satellite campuses of Western universities sprung up all over the region and created an edge over state-run universities. There was distinctive trend for the elite campuses, coming out of what we would call research universities, to set up research activities.

The nature of institutions varies though there is a general trend to put all Western university branch campuses in the region in a common basket. The structure, governance and mobilization of capital in each university differ from other. On the basis of ownership, branch campuses can be put in different categories. They can be owned solely by a foreign university or jointly between a foreign university and a local partner.[30] The ownership also varies from individuals to organizations and governments. Some of them like the American University of Kuwait are privately owned and intend to make a profit; others, such as the American University of Sharjah, are in public sector backed by members of the ruling family who cover their costs.[31] This means each of the Gulf countries follows a distinct pattern with regard to the establishment of private and foreign universities. GCC states in general exemplify three degrees of state control over higher education. In Qatar, funding for infrastructure development even for foreign universities remains to be the responsibility of the state through Qatar Foundation. Clearly

28. Linda Nording, "Gulf Universities Hope for Research Funds", *Nature* 27 (October 2011)
29. Ibid.
30. Wilkins, "Who Benefits from Foreign Universities in the Arab Gulf States?", 73.
31. James Calderwood "Western Universities Opening in GCC at Risk of Failing", *The National* 10 (April 2012).

differentiating the realm of state-funded and private, other GCC states such as UAE and Kuwait maintain a different practice. In Dubai, though it provides land, subsidies and special economic zone status to the foreign universities, the state keeps itself away from other financial involvements. Financial responsibility in that case is more asymmetrical, as these branches are expected to cover their own costs in what is designed as a co-investment operation. The establishment of private universities in Saudi is a recent development as the country showed a reluctance to allow private universities for several decades.

Within the UAE, there are actually two different models; the Abu Dhabi model and the Sharjah model.[32] The major difference is with regard to the academic involvement of foreign firms and scholars in the higher education. Sharjah has stimulated the growth of its universities with the aid of consultants from North America, but the result is an array of distinguished indigenous institutions with less external influence and control.[33] Universities in Abu-Dhabi have from the outset appointed mainly American academics in all leading positions.[34] In Saudi Arabia and Oman a distinctive model was developed with private stakeholders from within the country also were given maximum priority. A royal decree was issued in Oman in 1996 in order to promote the development of private higher educational institutions. Omani government and Omani citizens hold the ownership of most of the private higher educational institutions as the internationalization of higher education in the country is normally limited to certain joint enterprises with international support mostly from the UK, the US, Australia

32. Roderick French, "United Arab Emirates (UAE): Flagship of the Gulf", *Middle East Institute Viewpoints: Higher Education and the Middle East* 36 (May 2009), 13-15.
33. Ibid.
34. Ibid.

and New Zealand.[35]

Looking at the orientation, one can see there are two patterns of academic reform has been accepted in the Gulf[36]; either market-driven (like in Dubai), or state-driven (like in Saudi Arabia). By founding world-class, top-ranking universities, political leadership in Dubai seeks not just to fill the 'academic gap' in their countries; but explicitly intend to exploit the real estate value of such projects. The crisis in real estate sector has, therefore, badly affected the prospectus of such projects. For the government in Dubai private and foreign university projects become market-oriented reforms that have certain monitory advantages.[37] The establishment of new globalizing knowledge zones with multiple institutions from different countries brought together within them represents an explicit adoption of American style.[38] Over the last several years there is the emergence of such new knowledge spaces, totally different from traditional knowledge producers (and associated stakeholders) who have dominated the local higher education landscape.

Of the Arab Gulf states, three places of especially flourishing academic activity with major knowledge based economy projects are Qatar, the UAE, and Saudi Arabia.

2.1 Knowledge Village Dubai

Knowledge Village (KV) launched in 2003 was founded as a business entity of Dubai TECOM Free Zone. With founding the KV, the Dubai administration was in a way recreating the success of California's Silicon Valley by attracting a large number of famous international universities, professional

35. Donn and Al-Manthri, *Globalization and Higher Education in the Arab Gulf States*, 111.
36. Romani, "The Politics of Higher Education in the Middle East".
37. Ibid., 5.
38. Ibid.

training centers, and research and development centers from around the world.[39] As a free zone, the KV offers world-class amenities and services to its business partners including complete foreign ownership, total exemption from taxes, full repatriation of capital and profits, as well as smooth incorporation and visa issuance procedures.[40] The KV hosts over 450 companies, comprising a variety of knowledge-based business entities that range from training and development centers to human resources management and consultancy services. Within one year of inception, the KV had attracted 15 regional and international universities from nine different countries including Australia, India, Pakistan, Iran, Russia, Belgium, the UK, Ireland, and Canada.

2.2 International Academic City (Dubai)

Dubai International Academic City was launched in 2007 as a free zone connected to the knowledge village and dedicated exclusively to international higher education, where educational institutions from Dubai Knowledge Village moved to. DAC currently hosts 32 campus branches from 13 different countries. These branches include leading Western universities like Michigan State University from the US, the University of Wollongong & Murdoch University from Australia, Middlesex University and Heriot-Watt University from the UK.[41]

2.3 Education City (Doha)

This is an initiative of Qatar Foundation housing branch campuses of some of the world's leading Western universities. Education City aims to make Doha an epicenter

---

39. See the official website of the Knowledge Village, www.kv.ae (Accessed on 10 April 2013).
40. Ibid.
41. See the official website of International Academic City (Dubai), http://www.diacedu.ae (accessed on 10 April 2013).

of educational excellence in the region. Presently, seven US universities, one UK University, two Australian and one French University have branch campuses at Education City.[42] In contrast to Dubai's knowledge village, there is a profound commitment from the state through Qatar foundation in the form of substantial subsidies and incentives to the participating institutions.

2.4 King Abdullah University of Science and Technology (KAUST)

KAUST in Saudi Arabia is an individual campus project started in 2009. This is an international graduate-level research university dedicated to advancing science and technology. KAUST which is claimed to be the sixth richest in the world has recruited faculty from many of the best universities and research institutions in the world. With the establishment of KAUST, Saudi has set its plan to change the country from a site for knowledge reception to one of knowledge production.[43]

42. For details, see the official website of Education City (Qatar), www.myeducationcity.com (accessed on 10 April 2013).
43. See the official website of KAUST, http://www.kaust.edu.sa (accessed on 10 April 2013).

3

Why They are Attractive?

The establishment of foreign universities involves several economic and social considerations and Gulf governments find them attractive for several reasons.

3.1 Economic Reasons

1. Economically speaking, apart from providing educational opportunities for citizens and no-citizens alike foreign universities potentially generate non-oil revenue.[44] The governments in the GCC countries realized that "the long-term economic growth in the region will be achieved only through the development of a knowledge society."[45] Higher education, they felt is one of the major focal points of non-oil development and a catalyst to create a knowledge-based economy. It is of particular importance to the rulers of the United Arab Emirates, where the state depend heavily on expatriate manpower.
2. The marketization of education is by and large seen as

---

44. Neha Vohra, "Globalized Higher Education in the United Arab Emirates-unexpected Outcomes",http://globalhighered.wordpress.com/2008/06/25/globalized-higher-education-uae/ (accessed on 10 April) & Romani, "The Politics of Higher Education in the Middle East", 4.
45. United Nations Development Programme (UNDP), *Arab Human Development Report 2003.*

a new economic avenue by the governments in the GCC states. They welcome the contemporary commodification of higher education, part of which is indexed by the increasingly transnational nature of universities and the neoliberal orientation of international curricula.[46]

3. When the Gulf nationals prefer to study at branch campuses of international universities in their home countries, it offers a financial relief for the governments in the GCC States as they do not have to pay the tuition fees or bear the cost of students' education abroad.[47]
4. Foreign universities are also attractive to expatriates, who have limited access to the state-run educational institutions. The proliferation of such institutions means that a large number of expatriate middle-class children, who used to have to go abroad for higher education (usually to India, Australia, Canada, the US, or the UK), are increasingly able to stay in the Gulf States through the time of their college graduation.[48] With international branch campuses, Gulf expatriates are able to acquire a high quality internationally recognized degree at lower cost.[49]
5. In addition, in most Western countries, international students' tuition fees and cost of living are increasing, thus creating another barrier to overseas education.

---

46. Vohra, "Globalized Higher Education in the United Arab Emirates – unexpected Outcomes"
47. Wilkins, "Who Benefits from Foreign Universities in the Arab Gulf States?", 77.
48. First, between 25% and 75% of the population of the various GCC countries are foreign expatriates, an increasing proportion of who have the wealth and will to provide their children with high-quality national or international higher education in their host countries. See Romani, "The Politics of Higher Education in the Middle East", 4.

3.2 Non-Economic Reasons

1. The Governments in the GCC states recognized that many academic institutions in the Arab world, with few exceptions, are failing to produce enough qualified graduates with skills that serve the needs of the emerging economy.[50]
2. The lack of quality higher education institutions, together with the shortage of research opportunities, meant that the region was losing many of its students, who would travel overseas in search of better educational opportunities.
3. Since the tragic events of September 11th, the Arab Gulf region has witnessed a phenomenal drop in number of students applying to US universities due to the tightening of immigration security procedures. Hence many more of them prefer to study in their home countries.
4. Female students in certain GCC states are not allowed to study abroad on their own and many others prefer to study locally due to cultural constrains. One can expect that these new high-quality universities will be primarily attended by female students who were formerly prevented from studying abroad by conservative norms. More recently, specific female-only institutions have been established in some of the Gulf countries.
5. Gaining a degree from an internationally renowned foreign university off-campuses, boost future employment prospects of young people and give them an opportunity to study in a multi-cultural

---

49. Wilkins, "Who Benefits from Foreign Universities in the Arab Gulf States?", 78.
50. Romani, "The Politics of Higher Education in the Middle East", 2.

environment.

6. Finally, there is an element of prestige. As the students pick up mannerisms, styles and concepts directly from the educators, parents (both citizens and expatriates) whose children are taught by the westerners take it a matter of high esteem.

Foreign university branch campuses, of course, have augmented the higher education in the Gulf by increasing the opportunity of nationals for quality education of international standards. However, the newfound enthusiasm shown by the GCC governments in bringing in foreign universities doesn't create resonance among students. No doubt that the number of 'branch campuses' has exploded in the Gulf region over the past two decades. But what we seem to be witnessing is a reverse trend. A local survey report clearly indicates the reality that the Western universities lose appeal and students are no longer interested in studying in these institutions.[51] The survey finds ninety nine per cent of students believe the conditions at these universities are tough and cannot be met.[52] Another forty nine per cent found it extremely difficult to become part of the Western life and culture. Forty one per cent of the students said their families will never let them join Western universities. Twenty five per cent of the students found the current international political situation and the way the foreign students are treated do not encourage the students to enter Western universities.[53]

---

51. The study was conducted by the Shaikh Saqr Government Excellence Programme and it highlighted a lack of enthusiasm towards Western universities. For further details, N. Nazzal, "Dubai, A Hub for Higher Education", *Gulf News,* 27 February 2012.
52. Andrew Ross, "Human Rights, Academic Freedom, and Offshore Academics", http://www.aaup.org/AAUP/pubsres/academe/2011/JF/feat/ross.htm (accessed on 10 April 2011).
53. Ibid.

According to Willoughby, "there are important institutional, political and social challenges being faced by the new higher education institutions of the GCC."[54] Some of the prestigious institutions that opened in the region, according to him, are having difficulty recruiting quality students and rely on government subsidies. There are disturbing stories that suggest that many of the less prestigious institutions are under considerable financial stress. Closure of George Mason University in Ras al Khaimah in 2009 and cancellation of undergraduate programmes at Michigan State University in Dubai in the following year illustrate the situation better. There are also concerns about the inability of Gulf-based branch campuses not living up to the standards of home institution.[55]

54. John Willoughby, as quoted in Calderwood "Western Universities Opening in GCC at Risk of Failing".
55. Davidson, *Higher Education in the Gulf: Building Economies, Politics and Culture*, 36.

4

Manifestations of Orientalism

Orientalism in its simplest definition is the problematized way through which the Western scholars look in to the eastern societies, their cultures and historical past.[56] Being an ideology, Orientalism represents a discourse of Western domination and hegemony. In such discourse, the eastern societies, geographies, histories and cultures enjoy an assumed inferiority before the Western models. Orientalism as an academic paradigm helps one to explain, how the point of view or gaze of Western societies did determine the eastern societies, their cultures and knowledge systems. Edward Said points out to the power of Western discourses to create regimes of truth that marginalize or silence other discourses. Orientalism, according to him, sometimes turns out to be racism of a deceptively subtle kind, and he sought to demonstrate its pervasiveness and continuity especially since the time of European Enlightenment.[57] Said included scholarly orientalism in his scope, and even accorded it a crucial role in disseminating orientalist ideas in academia all over the world. Through an avalanche of literatures that bear the seal of post-colonialism the scholars have exposed various problems related to the Western way in looking at the societies of the east, though the Western understanding and representation of the East have grown ever more

56. Edward Said, *Orientalism* (London: Vintage Books, 1979).
57. Ibid.

nuanced, and diverse.

The manifestation of orientalism in the case of branch campus of Western universities in the Gulf often starts with the special treatment being enjoyed by the Gulf-based projects for accommodating foreign universities such as Education City in Qatar and Knowledge Village in Dubai. This issue is particularly significant when the governments in the region provides tremendous amount of financial and administrative support in the form of distribution of land, working capital and subsidies while the state universities face huge funding crisis. As Therin points out, through generous grants the governments in some GCC states created interesting financial conditions and academic ambience for foreign providers, who are more than happy to benefit when there are difficult times at home.[58] The governments in the Gulf offer plots of land for the construction of branch campuses, special grants for acquiring resources and loans with highly subsidized interest rates (Wilkins 2011: 79). In Qatar, there is a criticism against the preferential treatment given to elite Western educational institutions like Georgetown University, while state-run Qatar University faces a state of neglect in terms of state funding (2011: 81). Despite being funded fully or partly by the state, the intake of national students is relatively less in foreign university branch campuses. Local students constitute only a small proportion at New York University Abu Dhabi, even if this branch campus is wholly funded by the Abu Dhabi government (2011). New York University off-campus claims to recruit students globally in order to maintain the standard of parent institution (2011: 6). So is the case with the US universities in Qatar which are established with generous financial back up from Qatar Foundation. These universities

58. herin, "Gulf: When will its Higher Education models Implode?", 18.

enjoy structural and operational autonomy especially when it comes to matters like curriculum development, decision-making and students' admission.

The special stature being given to them involves two major considerations. Firstly, these mega educational projects are meant mainly for a spectacular display; not meant for the use of people in most of the cases. Secondly, being removed from the control of local governments, such spaces have acquired immunity from the rules of the land. They are the zones of neoliberal freedom and exception. Such cities do not conform to the laws of the land in areas such as employment and visa requirements, labor market-nationalization policies, or media infrastructure and censorship. With their autonomous stature, these universities have command over a wide range of affairs including financial regulations in the region and labor issues.[59] Otherwise complex issues like project licensing and nationalization of workforce become non-issues for them. It may be argued that internationalization has elevated higher education in the Gulf States to new international standards, but earning profit is the key motive for many of the projects, especially, when their parent institutions are faced with no or declined state funding in the home countries.

As specially administered areas, economic zones in the region in general have a different structure of governance and accountability. This extraterritorial nature the "special economic zone" with huge amount of immunity from national regulation has been extended to foreign university projects also. As a free zone, the Knowledge Village offers world-class amenities and services to its business partners including complete foreign ownership, total exemption from

59. M.H. Ilias, "New Market Spaces and Challenges to the State Sovereignty in the Arab Gulf Region", in Gulshan Dietl (ed.), *Democracy and Democratization in the Gulf* (New Delhi: Shipra Publications, 2010).

taxes, full repatriation of capital and profits, as well as smooth incorporation and visa issuance procedures.[60] With peculiar features of exemption and immunity, such zones replace the traditional 'unprofanable' or sacred spaces' of religion. Sacred spaces may be, therefore, read, not only as divine or religious, but also as the reflections and reproductions of social, political or economic desires. Agamben points out this aspect of sacredness and opens up the possibilities of extending the site of analysis beyond conventional sacred spaces.[61] For him, every object, which is placed in a separate sphere and kept far from popular use, is 'sacred'. Removing commodities largely from the popular use, capitalism also shows the salience of sacredness. It is therefore important to analyze the 'entrepreneurial, social, political and other 'profane forces' that constitute the construction of sacred space.

This analogy between sacred spaces of religion and market becomes very apparent while analyzing the nature of organization and the kind of immunity being enjoyed by both the conventional sacred spaces of religion and the new ones of knowledge economy. Both are allowed to be operated somewhat freely within the state and are seldom liable to the political and legal constrains. The knowledge based special economic zones in the Gulf region in particular are specific areas that have special laws and nature of governance different from and more liberal than a country's typical ones. One of the most noticeable illustrations of this issue is in Saudi Arabia, where the proposed site for Knowledge Economic City is nowhere other than Medina, which is supposed to be one among the two 'holiest' cities for Muslims.

---

60. For details, see the official website of the Knowledge Village, www.kv.ae (Accessed on 10 April 2013).
61. Georgio Agamben, *Profanations* (New York: Zone Books, 2007).

5

Ethno-Centric Recruitment System

Another major avenue where the issue of orientalism has a clear ramification is the recruitment drive in which preference is generally being given to European or North American applicants. A close examination of the situation vacant advertisements appeared on the official websites of the new generation universities would reveal the practice of Euro-centrism in a subtle manner. Academics at international off-campuses often enjoy a lot of privileges and work in a resource-rich environment. The packages offered to them are often all-inclusive comprising an attractive remuneration, accommodation, tax free salary and other incentives. Teaching positions in many of the disciplines are frankly not meant for Asians and Africans but for Western Europeans, North Americans or Western educated non-GCC Arabs who enjoy certain special status and occupy the lucrative positions. Even the Gulf nationals are often provided with managerial or administrative support roles.

With much more concerned over projecting a 'global' image, state universities always import British, Canadian and Australian teachers. These institutions sometimes complain that it is hard to recruit the academics of same quality at their branch campuses as they do at parent institutions.[62]

---

62. John Gill, "The Perils of Joining the Gulf Rush", *Times Higher Education* 9 (December 2012).

Employing South and Southeast Asian teachers is often being viewed as an act of lowering academic standards among the local students who preserve a strong stereotype image (of low grade employees, house drivers and office boys) of these populations in their mind. Teachers from India often manage to get a Western university tag in order to overcome this ethno-centric taboo. The division is becoming more profound with the universities' effort to institutionalize the discrimination on the basis of nationality with unequal compensation structure. The staff and faculty pay structures are still nationality or ethnicity-based. For the same job, South Asians are being paid less than the Europeans or the Arabs from Egypt, Jordan and Lebanon. Recruitment in Saudi universities may be an exceptional case where there is a massive employment of Indian teachers, despite the pressure emanating from Saudization.[63]

Employment website of American University in Dubai clearly says that candidates for certain positions should have a Western university degree.[64] More recently, the UAE University has intensified its recruitment of Americans to the faculty and to senior academic administrative positions. Most strikingly, the Ministry recently announced that they will seek full institutional accreditation for UAEU from one of the US regional associations.[65] This thoroughgoing

---

63. Although the targeted nationalization remains active, mismatching profiles of nationals and monetary concerns over the employment of European teachers have hindered the removal of Indians in university teaching positions in Saudi Arabia. The progress has, of course, been made to replace South Asian workforce with nationals in certain areas of employment, large scale removal of them in the colleges, universities and hospitals seems difficult.
64. See the official website of American University, http://www.aud.edu/About_AUD/HR/hr.asp (accessed on 10 April 2013).
65. French, "United Arab Emirates",13.

"Americanization" of a sovereign nation's federal education system is closely parallel everywhere and has a spillover effect in other emirates also. For more than a decade, Zayed University in Abu-Dhabi and Qatar University have invested heavily in US and UK consulting teams, obtaining advice from them on matters like curriculum design and staff appointment. The three leading emirates in the UAE involved in this enterprise are Abu Dhabi, Dubai and Sharjah. The hallmark of reform and expansion in all three cases has been Americanization, but the distinct differences in the models adopted by the three governments are in themselves instructive.[66]

The peculiar architectural designs of some of these universities that follow the Western style blindly are also reflective of some oriental imagination. The specific European architecture of Sorbonne University Campus in Abu-Dhabi is a handbook sort of example for such a blind adoption.

66. Ibid.

6

Text Books and Curriculum

The adoption of Western style education, practices, textbooks, and educators in the Gulf in various ways bring their own models to the classroom and into the learning process. Adopting Western style education is claimed to give students the opportunity to gain some perspective on Western culture, which help minimize differences and bridge gaps of understanding. But what happens in most of the cases is simply opposite to what the governments and the foreign institutions expect. The students show a tendency to merely mimic the mannerisms of their instructors rather than understanding the culture of west or cultivating fresh outlooks to look their own culture. Similarly, the knowledge acquired contradicts what they've learned naturally and sometime goes against the cultural norms. The collective preference for teaching in English with Western-oriented coursework also gives Western academics an advantage over nationals. Some of the Western modeled practices which may fit into the particular European context do not sit well with the conservatives in the region. These criticisms imply that many of the higher-education experiments sweeping through the region are culturally insensitive and academically inappropriate. It raises a genuine question how could the cultural ethos of European societies possibly thrive in the Gulf?

In the name of introducing a curriculum politically and culturally sensitive to the nation, the humanities, social sciences, and liberal arts are not developed in the Gulf.[67] Teaching of politics, religion and culture can all be affected by local sensitivities. Same sort of complications occur with regard to the teaching of local history. With highly sensitive contents, history of various tribal groups remains a taboo subject for expatriate teachers to engage in.[68] So is always the case with domestic political systems also. That tradition, however, gets gradually vanished as a handful of universities offer course in such sensitive disciplines. Indigenous universities pioneered this trend with developing authentic studies of their own societies. Sultan Qabus University established Omanis Studies Centre in 1998. Qatar University recently launched Master's Programme in Gulf Studies. The American University of Kuwait recently started the country's first course in Gulf history. The students who wish to study such disciplines used to go abroad to do so. Until recently, the larger instances of overseas involvement in the Gulf States have been limited to specific programs, and in disciplines—such as engineering, business, and medicine—that do not usually attract much intolerance from the host society.[69] The expected focus of the new curricula is always to domesticate social sciences within a framework of social engineering. The curriculum is carefully designed not to challenge the national polity and foster critical thinking. The issue is a sensitive one as local governments paying for student's degrees expect to see state's benefit in promoting foreign universities.

The traditional focus on business and management degrees in the region reflects the interests of the local governments and teaching these disciplines becoming more of a political priority in the Gulf countries. A recent statistics shows that seventy four per cent of the Emirati students

67. Romani, "The Politics of Higher Education in the Middle East", 5.
68. Davidson, *Higher Education in the Gulf*, 5.
69. Ibid.

studying in Bachelors programmes have opted Business Studies as major.[70]

Similarly, there is a trend to equate higher education with gaining diploma in technical education and there is little concern about the research. Importance of knowledge production in the institutions of higher learning remains poorly understood, when education is highly commercialized. Programmes being offered at the college and university levels are market-friendly with aim to contribute to the country's economic development as well as reducing youth unemployment.[71] Similarly, most of the foreign higher education institutions concentrate on European language learning programmes with a declared aim of making the students exposed to the 'global' languages. This may help students who need to learn English or French before entering into the job market. But, the lack of enthusiasm in teaching Arabic at the higher level may lead to issues with serious cultural repercussions.

It is true that the foreign universities have improved the skills and employability of the nationals entering the labour market. Students pass out from these institutions are well absorbed in the public and private sector firms. However, a report on higher education shows that there is serious lack of institutions promoting research and a miniscule few of only 0.1 per cent of students go for doctoral research in the GCC states.[72] Over importance given to developing technical skills and substituting English for Arabic as the medium of instruction leave initiatives for understanding own culture, history and civilization unattended. There is an extremely opposite trend to self-censor-showing over-sensitiveness to the local culture. Some institutions, for instance, do not use

70. Nazzal, "Dubai, A Hub for Higher Education".
71. Wilkins,"Who Benefits from Foreign Universities in the Arab Gulf States?", 75.
72. Nazzal, "Dubai, A Hub for Higher Education".

art books that depict the human body, a practice that is considered un-Islamic.[73] To quote Ghabra: "rather than being insensitive, the new institutions' tendency to self-censor is affecting their standards."[74]

Text books and course materials in most of the cases become the finest examples of the plain subscription of oriental perspectives. Western universities often rely on imported teaching materials often from UK, US, Canada, France and Australia. One can argue that the situation was not very different earlier as the institutions of higher learning were depended wholly on teaching materials and text books imported from Egypt, Syria and Lebanon. But the course materials imported from Europe and North America sometimes contain case studies and examples not entirely compatible with the experiences of Gulf societies. The way through which these text books look into the eastern societies and their cultures is always problematic and provides case studies to understand how 'orientalism revisits in academic discourse. The textbooks that used in classrooms do not have enough connection to local society. As Rogmans notes, "some undergraduate classes use the US textbooks that include whole chapters about US politics and legislation."[75]

Another major issue to be discussed in this context is the subtle racial discrimination shown towards the Asian student communities. Scholars like Vora have pointed out that the social, cultural, geographic, and work spaces of different communities are very segregated and defined by systemic inequalities in these universities.[76] It is a fact that class,

73. Ibid.
74. Shafeeq Ghabra as quoted in Claderwood, "Western Universities Opening in GCC at Risk of Failing".
75. Tim Rogmans, as quoted in Claderwood, "Western Universities Opening in GCC at Risk of Failing".
76. Vohra, "Globalized Higher Education in the United Arab Emirates".

ethnicity and nationality determine the spatial distribution of people in the region. The housing pattern is highly segregated with specially designated areas or exclusive enclaves for locals and each category of expatriates. Western universities modeled on European and American institutions are the spaces supposed to have people placed on equal footing, at least theoretically. However, the practice sometimes contradicts the claim.

Taking cue from the experiences of South Asian students, Vora points out that there is a systemic but subtle discrimination against them in these universities.[77] It is a fact that students from the expatriate communities (mainly Indian Pakistani ad Iranian) constitute the majority of student population in international branch campuses in UAE and Qatar.[78] But the numerical strength seldom reflects in the treatment being given to them. Even though they study in a very international space, many South Asian students have shared their experience of exclusion with the author while doing a field study. There is a hierarchy based on the nationality and ethnic origin. The upper stratum is composed of GCC Arab students combined with those who come from North America and Europe. The non-GCC Arab students who share many things in common with the natives also enjoy certain special status and the middle stratum is comprised mainly of them. South Asian, South East Asian and African students have a clear perception of their status in this hierarchy.

---

77. Ibid.
78. L.W. Foderaro, "NYU Abu Dhabi Scours Globe for Top Students", *The New York Times*, 20 June 2010.

7

Conclusion

With bringing more and more Western universities to the Gulf soil, the governments in the GCC countries explicitly intend to reverse the balance of knowledge between the West and West Asia. Governments invest in the foreign university projects in the hope of turning their revenues from oil into human capital to grow a more durable knowledge based economy. The establishment of off-campuses of the international universities, of course, has considerably reduced massive outflow of GCC students to go abroad for higher studies. As the Gulf States have had a lack of competent institutions of higher learning, thousands of students had enrolled at overseas universities every year.

The GCC States also have benefited out of foreign university branch campuses as they have improved the knowledge and skills of young people and thereby improved the employability of them. This has, in a way, helped transform Gulf countries to increase the pace of labour market nationalization and to reduce youth unemployment. The contribution of branch campuses of international universities to the effort of Gulf governments to transform their economies to knowledge-based economy is worth-mentioning. Gaining a more 'highly respected' foreign degree boosts future employment prospects of them.

However, some recent works reveal that the situation is not very bright as being portrayed outside and the Gulf States' effort to develop regional hubs for higher education by attracting more international universities is not without challenges (Donn and Al-Manthri: 2010). While the declared aim is the emergence of the Arab Gulf as a heavyweight academic actor in the region, it is seen by some as further intrusion of the West and yet another cycle of Western intellectual domination in the region. Anyway, the process of implementation of foreign higher education model within the local context is more problematic and challenging than anticipated at the planning stages.

The system of learning, curriculum and even the text books give Western academics an advantage over nationals. Many of the practices in higher education sweeping through the region become culturally insensitive. Lacking emphasis on critical thinking they adopt a different pedagogy alien to the practices prevailing at their home campuses. Likewise, the present importation of Western models represents a sudden shift that subscribes to a market-friendly view seeing education as a commodity that can be produced and consumed as per the demands of market. As the biggest task for higher education set by the governments in the Gulf is technical skill development, the branch-campuses focus mainly on programs that are required by the labour market and seldom concentrate on fostering critical thinking. And there is a tendency to see higher education as a major catalyst to achieve labour market nationalization and increased diversity in economics. Branch campuses of international universities also endorse this view without much of hassles.

Disciplines like business administration, banking, engineering, computer sciences and health sciences enjoy special attention, while social science and humanities face a Cinderella treatment. With a vision to transform country's education system and build a knowledge economy, the government in each GCC state offers the foreign universities a plethora of building grants, tax incentives, subsidies and guaranteed students numbers. This special treatment also engenders some serious political and social considerations.

And it raises a perplexing question to what extent are the regimes in Gulf prepared to absorb, and cope with the social consequences that these foreign university projects create within the country.

References

Agamben, Georgio. *Profanations*. New York: Zone Books, 2007.

Al-Khaldi, Salem. "Education Policies in the Gulf States", *Research Papers Series*. Dubai: Gulf Research Centre, January 2007.

P.G. Altbach. "Globalization and the University: Myths and Realities in an Unequal World", *Tertiary Education and Management* 10 (2004): 1-25.

Calderwood, James. "Western Universities Opening in GCC at Risk of Failing", *The National* 10, no.4 (2012): 18-26.

Davidson, Christopher. *Higher Education in the Gulf: Building Economies, Politics and Culture*. London: Saqi Books, 2008.

Donn, Gari and Al-Manthri, Yahya. *Globalization and Higher Education in the Arab Gulf States*. Dicot: Symposium Books, 2010.

Foderaro, L.W. "NYU Abu Dhabi Scours Globe for Top Students", *The New York Times*, 20 June 2010.

French, Roderick. "United Arab Emirates (UAE): Flagship of the Gulf", *Middle East Institute Viewpoints: Higher Education and the Middle East* 36 (May 2009): 13-15.

Gill, John. "The Perils of Joining the Gulf Rush", *Times Higher Education* 9 (December 2012).

Ilias, M.H. "New Market Spaces and Challenges to the State Sovereignty in the Arab Gulf Region", in Dietl Gulshan, ed. *Democracy and Democratization in the Gulf*, 86-101. New Delhi: Shipra Publications, 2010.

Krieger, Zvika. "Dubai, Aiming to Be an Academic Hub", *The Chronicle of Higher Education* 54 (October 2007): 12-16.

Nazzal, N. "Dubai: A Hub for Higher Education", *Gulf News*, 27 February 2012.

Nording, Linda. "Gulf Universities Hope for Research Funds", *Nature*, 27 October 2011.

Olcott, Don. "Emerging Opportunities and Challenges for Regional Higher Education", *Middle East Institute Viewpoints: Higher Education and the Middle East* 36 (May 2011): 7-9.

Romani, Vincent. "The Politics of Higher Education in the Middle East: Problems and Prospects", *Middle East Institute Viewpoints: Higher Education and the Middle East* 36 (May 2009): 2-3.

Ross, Andrew. "Human Rights, Academic Freedom, and Offshore Academics", *http://www.aaup.org/AAUP/pubsres/academe/2011/JF/feat/ross.html.*

Said, Edward. *Orientalism.* London: Vinatge Books, 1979.

Therin, Francois. "Gulf: When will its Higher Education models Implode?", *University World News* 180 (2011): 17.

Vohra, Neha. "Globalized Higher Education in the United Arab Emirates – Unexpected Outcomes", http://globalhighered.wordpress.com/2008/06/25/globalized-higher-education-uae/.

Wilkins, Stephen. "Who Benefits from Foreign Universities in the Arab Gulf States?", *Australian Universities' Review* 53 (2011): 73-83.